For the squeaky-clean Cathie, well-groomed Jack,
and superbly combed Cathleen.

Library of Congress Cataloging-in-Publication Data available.
ISBN: 978-1-4521-0056-2

Book design by Amy Achaibou and Aimee Gauthier.
Typeset in Smiley.
The illustrations in this book were rendered in cut paper, ribbon, and pastel.

Manufactured by Toppan Leefung, Da Ling Shan Town, Dongguan, China, in June 2011.

1 3 5 7 9 10 8 6 4 2

This product conforms to CPSIA 2008.

Chronicle Books LLC
680 Second Street, San Francisco, California 94107

www.chroniclekids.com

FSC
www.fsc.org
MIX
Paper from
responsible sources
FSC® C104723

Animal Baths

By Bob Barner

chronicle books · san francisco

Monkeys groom messy hair
to start the monkey day.

Elephants flap big ears
in cool, misty spray.

Ducks ruffle wet feathers as they wash, preen, and primp.

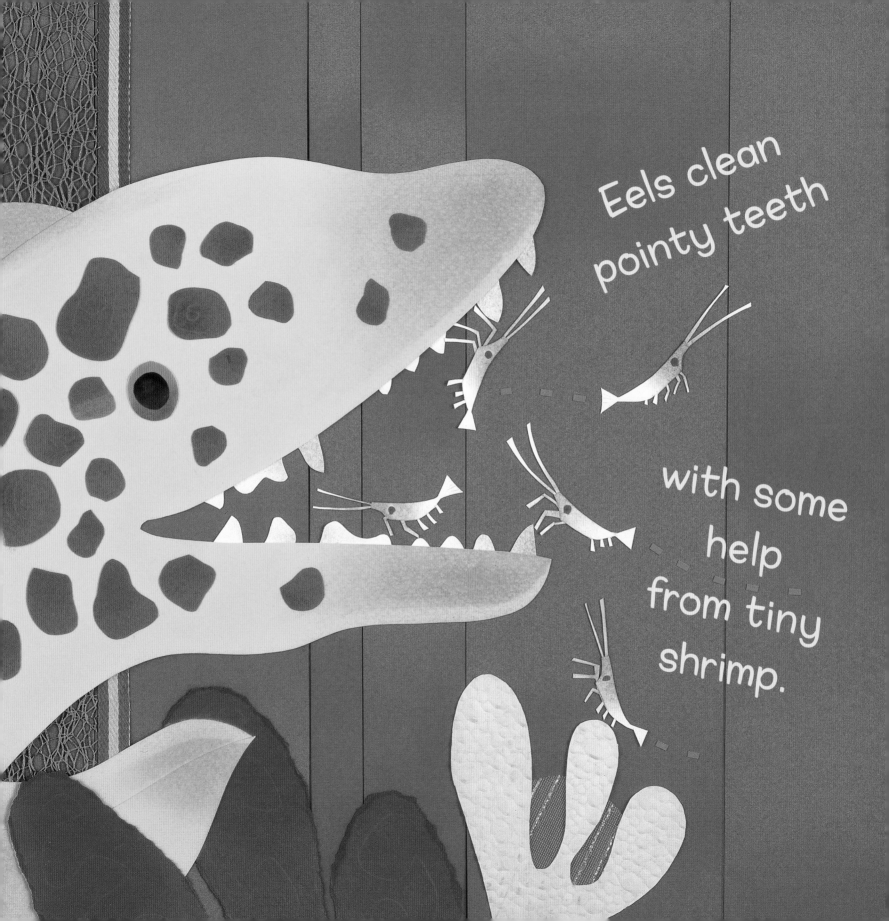

Eels clean pointy teeth with some help from tiny shrimp.

Pigs wallow over itches
in a muddy pool.

Manatees wait
to be cleaned
by a fishy school.

Bats keep wings
soft and neat

with lots of
little licks.

Bears scratch
against tall trees

to rub off
mud and ticks.

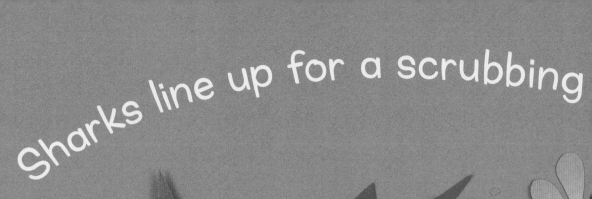

Sharks line up for a scrubbing

and a gentle check.

Giraffes stretch long necks
as birds nip pests with a peck.

Animals like to get clean
just like you and me.

When you take a bath today,
which one will you be?

Comb your messy hair
like the monkeys do.

Wash your elephant
ears with nice shampoo.

Clean up like a duck when
you preen and primp.

Brush your teeth with no
help from tiny shrimp.

Wallow like a pig
in a sudsy pool.

Wash your face and hands
when you go to school.

Scrub with a cloth like
a bat in a rush.

Scratch your itchy skin
with a bristle brush.

Wait while Mom gives your
sharky skin a check.

Clean up your dirty hands,
feet, and long neck.